THE
WORLD
REDUCED TO
INFOGRAPHICS

THE
WORLD
REDUCED TO
INFOGRAPHICS

**From Hollywood's Life Lessons and Doomed Cities of the U.S.
to Sociopathic Cats and What Your Drink Order Says About You**

Worm Miller and Patrick Casey

 Ulysses Press

Published by:
ULYSSES PRESS
P.O. Box 3440
Berkeley, CA 94703
www.ulyssespress.com

ISBN: 978-1-56975-989-9
Library of Congress Catalog Number 2011926036

Printed in the United States by Bang Printing

10 9 8 7 6 5 4 3 2 1

Acquisitions editor: Keith Riegert
Managing editor: Claire Chun
Editor: Lauren Harrison
Proofreader: Abigail Reser
Cover design: what!design @ whatweb.com
Graphs: Marek Haiduk
Interior clip art: page 47 © Black Images/shutterstock.com; page 76 © NEV/shutterstock.com; page 94 © Yalik/shutterstock.com; page 116 © veselin gajin/shutterstock.com; page 118 © Alexander A. Sobolev/shutterstock.com

Distributed by Publishers Group West

For Candice

CONTENTS

INFOGRAPHICS:
AN INTRODUCTION TO LEARNING

Confucius famously wrote, "You cannot open a book without learning something." Yeah, right. Give it a shot. Pull the nearest book from your shelf, open it to any random page, and stare blankly at it. Learn anything? Chances are you'll glean nothing; at best you'll have spent a relaxing moment in thoughtless meditation. Confucius may have offered us some theoretically sage advice, but in this case he was wrong. Despite his wisdom, he ignored two diametrically opposed facts of human nature:

1. People like knowing things.
2. People hate learning things.

Thus enters our answer to Confucius's flawed theory: a book composed entirely of single-page information morsels. Revolutionizing the field of illustrative epistemology (the study of picture-based knowledge), we have crafted a tome of anthropological, sociological, and philosophical superknowledge, all easily absorbed while taking a short break from your busy day or using the toilet.

Illustrative epistemologists believe that how we transfer knowledge from one person to the next is the very essence of being human. Throughout our history, scientists and scholars from a host of fields have sought simple qualifiers to define humanity's uniqueness within the animal kingdom. Time and again, though, these supposedly singular traits have proven not so singular. Man, the toolmaker? Hardly. Egyptian vultures use rocks to crack open thick-shelled ostrich eggs. Man, the builder? Not quite. Pesky beavers were erecting elaborate dams long before we were. Man, the artist? Think again. Bowerbirds express their individuality by constructing extraordinarily lavish and often colorful nests. What about our singularly shameful attributes? Man, the wager of war? Relax. Chimpanzees have been known to invade and kill their neighbors for no other reason than to gain new territory.

Our species, *Homo sapiens*, is Latin for "knowing man" or "wise man," but even our noninstinctual knowledge crown has been usurped from us by a variety of species ranging from apes to monkeys to dolphins to whales, which have been witnessed passing newly acquired knowledge from generation to generation.

In the end, what may be our only truly singular qualifier is man, recorder of knowledge. A mother chimp may teach her children a special technique for retrieving termites from a mound using a stick, but were she to die before passing the skill along, the chain of knowledge would be broken. Only humans have devised ways for acquired knowledge to be passed beyond the limited reach of person-to-person interaction, and, more importantly, beyond the confines of our often too-brief life spans.

Unfortunately, the major knowledge-transfer systems, for all their positives, suffer from what scientists call the "Boredom Factor." They simply take too much time or effort away from the modern person's busy schedule of unhappy work and inane leisure distractions. Which is why illustrative epistemology champions the use of information graphics, or, shortened for increasingly shortened attention spans, infographics.

The infographic is a straightforward concept. It simply imparts information that would be cumbersome if rendered in mere text form. In our modern world, infographics are generally used as visual shorthand: street signs, mass-transit maps, which bathroom is meant for men and which is meant for women. Without these infographics, people die.

But the idea behind infographics can be traced back to our prehistory. Before humans had a written language, our Stone Age ancestors were documenting hunting adventures with paint on cave walls. The ancient Egyptians and Mesoamericans adorned their temples with narrative imagery. The Vikings left carved and painted rune stones across Europe, Iceland, Greenland, and northeastern North America documenting their travels. Scholars are just beginning to fully grasp the meanings behind much of this early visual data.

Confucius was taking for granted that people would actually read a book. Illustrative epistemologists recognize that left to their own devices, the average person is simply not going to engage recorded knowledge. After the rigorous tedium of a standard K–12 education, most people intentionally disengage from the learning process entirely, content with the assumption that they have acquired enough knowledge to suitably see them to the grave. Learning is a chore, and there are a lot of kittens that need your attention on the Internet.

With the infographic, however, before you even realize it, you've absorbed the information contained within it. The infographic is the Trojan horse of pedagogy. A stealth bomber with an explosive payload of pure data. A wet willy of knowledge inserted into the eager ear.

Our case rested, you should now prepare yourself for a mind-blowing knowledge experience. In your hands lies a staggering swath of modern human scientific and cultural knowledge condensed into one simple volume. If a picture is worth a thousand words, then this book is an entire set of the Encyclopaedia Britannica ready to fit snugly on the lid of your toilet tank.

Feed your mind.

Introduction
to Graphic Humor

Flowchart
(Processus cursus)

First introduced in 1921 by Frank Gilbreth Sr. to document process
flow in industrial engineering, the flowchart quickly became a popular
instructional tool in the industrial world (Post 1935). However, the
flowchart soon evolved from simply showing the steps of a structured
sequence to something akin to a hypothetical journey—a process made
up of variable steps with variable outcomes.

The flowchart's appeal is that of an expedition, an exploration. It's
all the fun of a *Choose Your Own Adventure*, but with the comfort of
fate controlling your course. Flowcharts have become a popular way to
visualize the possibilities of such critical situations as "You Are Lost in
the Desert" and "You Poured Cereal into a Bowl Before Checking to See
if You Had Milk."

What are you reading?

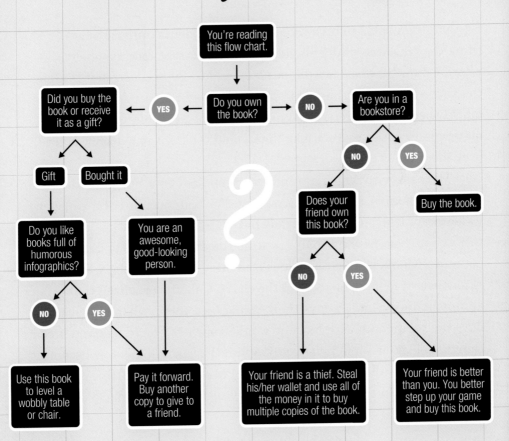

Line Graph
(At linea)

Easily recognizable to high school algebra students or those who think they're successfully playing the stock market, line graphs track relationships between two different variables. By marking points along the x axis and connecting those dots to form a line, trends and patterns quickly become apparent to even the untrained eye, often allowing observers to notice correlations that would otherwise have gone right over their heads.

The ease with which a trend can be spotted on a line graph has been integral to many important discoveries. For instance, in 1914, Giuseppe Calentori of Italy, a baker by trade but an infographic enthusiast by inclination, began a line chart tracking the daily number of fights he got into with his wife on the y axis compared to time on the x axis. After several months of keeping the chart, Calentori realized that approximately every 28 days there would be a spike, when for several days the arguments with his wife would come even more fast and furious than usual. After some investigation into the cause, Calentori became the first man to discover the concept of PMS (Calentori 1915). Women, of course, had been aware of their monthly cycles since the dawn of time.

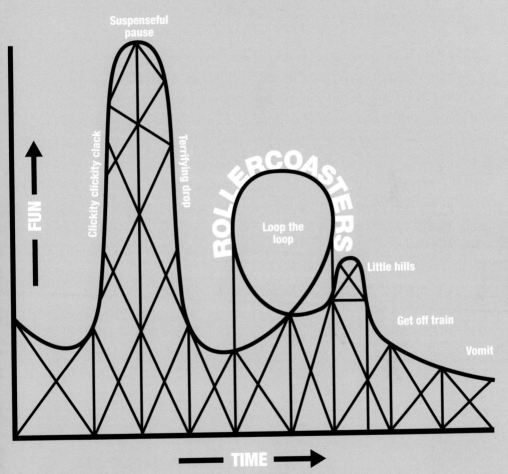

17

Vs. Chart

(Informatio bellum)

World War II hero General George S. Patton once said, "Battle is the most magnificent competition in which a human being can indulge" (Patton 1944). But the ancient Chinese general Sun Tzu said, "The supreme art of war is to subdue the enemy without fighting" (Sun Tzu [500 BC?]). In the world of infographics, we side with Sun Tzu. Everyone loves a good brawl, and what better way to satiate our bloodlust than in the bloodless arena of cold, hard facts and statistics. In such a hypothetical forum, we can pit individuals from varying time periods and realities against each other in gladiatorial sport, settling once and for all natural age-old rivalries, like, Who would win in a fight, Superman or Mighty Mouse?

(The answer, of course, is Superman. Mighty Mouse's weakness is Limburger cheese, which is much easier to acquire than Kryptonite. Also, Mighty Mouse is a mouse.)

BATTLE OF COLUMBUS

CHRISTOPHER COLUMBUS

Who: Explorer

1492: Year he set sail

Worst Crime:
Enslavement of Native Americans

Best Idea: Find another way to India

Biggest Achievement:
Colonization of the New World

Biggest Mistake:
Thought he'd reached India

Sweet Deal:
10% of Spain's profits from the New World (reneged)

CHRIS COLUMBUS

Who: Hollywood director

1492: Production company

Worst Crime: *Bicentennial Man*

Best Idea: *Gremlins*

Biggest Achievement:
Harry Potter

Biggest Mistake: Thought Macaulay Culkin would have a real career

Sweet Deal:
A percentage of the profits from the Harry Potter movies

Pie Chart
(Informatio circuli)

The pie chart, also known as the circle graph, is one of the most ubiquitous infographics in the world. Everyone loves pie, making the charts both easy to absorb and pleasant to imagine eating, which allows the delicious information or data filling to be all the more digestible.

Early forms of pie first appeared in Northern Africa around 9500 BC during the Egyptian Neolithic period, though the tasty pastry treat we think of when we hear the word *pie* did not appear until the ancient Greeks got hold of it (Zytho 1955). Pies were not employed in "chart" form until the Scottish political economist William Playfair published the book *Statistical Breviary* in 1801. Playfair later experimented with other possible food/chart combinations based on traditional Scottish cuisine, but his "black pudding table," "potted heid visual aid," and "haggis diagram" all proved significantly less appetizing and successful (Playfair 1804).

WHAT KINDS OF WORDS ARE ON URBAN DICTIONARY

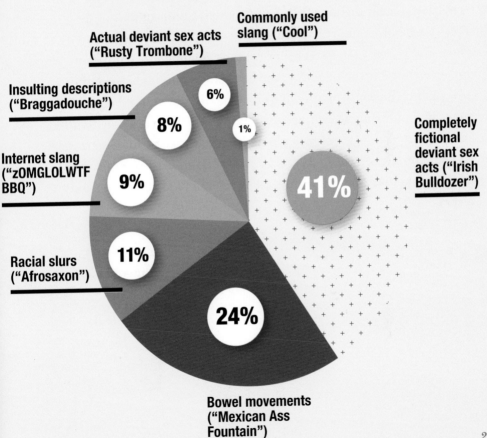

Actual deviant sex acts ("Rusty Trombone")

Commonly used slang ("Cool")

Insulting descriptions ("Braggadouche")

Internet slang ("zOMGLOLWTF BBQ")

Racial slurs ("Afrosaxon")

Completely fictional deviant sex acts ("Irish Bulldozer")

Bowel movements ("Mexican Ass Fountain")

6%

1%

8%

9%

11%

41%

24%

Venn Diagrams

Prior to 1880, the graphical world had no simple way to convey informational relationships. We could compare and contrast side-by-side data, but no chart existed that visually represented shared characteristics between two or more things. Then John Venn came along. Using everyone's favorite shape, the circle (or sometimes the circle's weird cousin, the oval), Venn devised an easily understood and instantly iconic system for diagramming overlapping relationships. Originally used by Venn as a way to teach elementary set theory, his diagram is most commonly used these days as a way to compare the unfavorable traits of celebrities and other humorous members of society on the Internet.

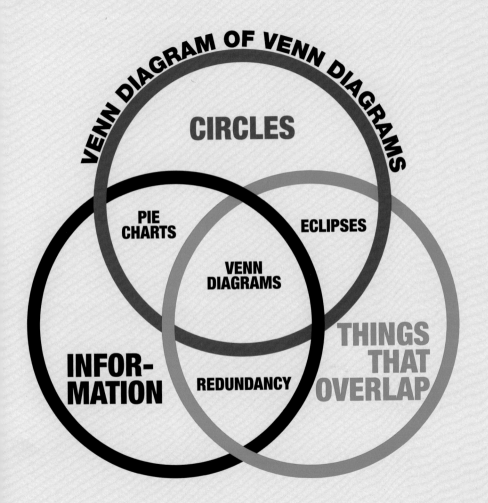

VENN DIAGRAM OF VENN DIAGRAMS

CIRCLES

PIE CHARTS

ECLIPSES

VENN DIAGRAMS

INFOR-MATION

REDUNDANCY

THINGS THAT OVERLAP

Science and the Terrifying Shit That Wants to Kill You

Science

Statistics indicate that scientists are no fun (Erinsen 1999). Scientists are always warning us that we're destroying the planet, that the things that we love are killing us, and that our archaic leech-based medical treatments aren't going to work. Well, we have one question for those scientists: How are we supposed to remove the evil spirits from our bodies if not with leeches? Huh? Not so smart now, are you?

If some of you are still interested in learning about science, you have the following options:

A. **Go to college.** *Time cost:* 4 years. *Money cost:* $120,000
B. **Read the following infographics.** *Time cost:* 10 minutes. *Money cost:* Price of book.

Choose wisely.

*The Periodic Table of the Elements
(c. AD 1500)*

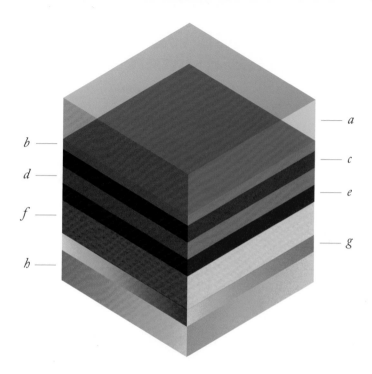

A Cross Section of Planet Earth

ⓐ Atmosphere
Oxygen, Nitrogen, Carbon Dioxide, Airplanes, Eagles

ⓑ Surface
Buildings, Trees, Girls, TVs

ⓒ Upper Monster Layer
C.H.U.D.s, Sewer Crocodiles

ⓓ Crust
Dirt, Rock, Buried Treasure, Corpses

ⓔ Lower Monster Layer
Mole People, Spice Worms, Morlocks

ⓕ Mantle
Dinosaur Bones, Crashed Alien Spacecraft, Slumbering Godzilla Foes

ⓖ Outer Core
Land That Time Forgot, Living Dinosaurs

ⓗ Inner Core
Bubble Gum, Tootsie Rolls

THINGS WE LIKE
VS. THE HUMAN BODY

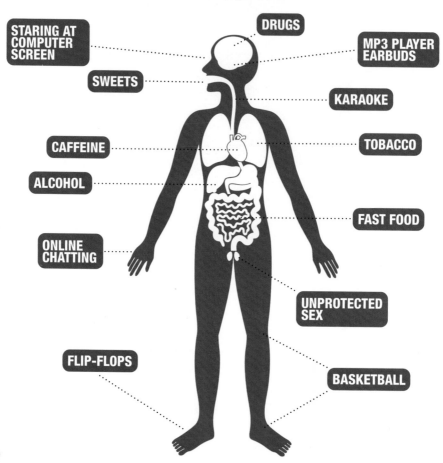

STARING AT COMPUTER SCREEN

DRUGS

MP3 PLAYER EARBUDS

SWEETS

KARAOKE

CAFFEINE

TOBACCO

ALCOHOL

ONLINE CHATTING

FAST FOOD

UNPROTECTED SEX

FLIP-FLOPS

BASKETBALL

SPIDER

Powers:
Sticky hands

Side effects:
Nocturnal web emissions

Weakness:
Rolled-up magazines

What you would call yourself:
Spider-Man

CAT

Powers:
Superior balance, night vision

Side effects:
Constant napping, increased vanity

Weakness:
Squirt gun

What you would call yourself:
Mister Meows

DOG

Powers:
Superior sense of smell, strong jaws

Side effects:
Desire to mark territory by peeing on everything

Weakness:
Desperate need for human attention

What you would call yourself:
The WereDog

HAMSTER

Powers:
Store things in cheeks

Side effects:
Random, inexplicable death

Weakness:
Easily trapped inside balls

What you would call yourself:
Ham Star

RADIOACTIVE ANIMAL BITE MUTATIONS

PENGUIN

Powers:
Hold breath, swim fast

Side effects:
Funny walk

Weakness:
Documentary filmmakers

What you would call yourself:
The Emperor

DOLPHIN

Powers:
Sonar sense, super healing abilities

Side effects:
Increased playfulness

Weakness:
Tuna nets

What you would call yourself:
The Splash

SKUNK

Powers:
Horrible, blinding farts

Side effects:
Near blindness, social outcast status

Weakness:
Rabies

What you would call yourself:
Stink Ray

31

A SHORT GUIDE TO BODILY FUNCTIONS

FART — FLATULENCE — CUT THE CHEESE

BELCH — ERUCTATION — REVIEW TODAY'S MENU

POOP — DEFECATION — PINCH A LOAF

PEE — URINATION — MAKE APPLE JUICE

VOMIT — EMESIS — TOSS COOKIES

- Colloquial Term
- Scientific Term
- Culinary Term

LEADING CAUSE OF HUMAN DEATHS BY WILD ANIMAL (GLOBAL)

KILLER WHALE
(SEA WORLD)

RAT
(EUROPE, MEDIEVAL)

SPIDER
(MEXICO)

SHARK
(FLORIDA)

TIGER
(INDIA)

CROCODILE
(SOUTHEAST ASIA)

VELOCIRAPTOR
(ISLA NUBLAR)

HIPPOPOTAMUS
(AFRICA)

JELLYFISH
(PHILIPPINES)

Zoological Guide to Suborder Caniformia

LATIN TERM	COMMON TERM	DESCRIPTION
Canis lupus domesticus	**Dog**	*Unattractive female*
Vulpes	**Fox**	*Attractive female*
Canis lupus	**Wolf**	*Predatory male*
Ursidae	**Bear**	*Large, bearded gay male*
Melinae	**Badger**	*Unattractive older female*
Odobenidae	**Walrus**	*Fat male with a mustache*
Mustela	**Weasel**	*Untrustworthy sleazeball*
Ailuropoda melanoleuca	**Panda**	*Person too nervous for sexual intercourse*
Phocidae	**Seal**	*Scarred, sweet-voiced crooner, often spotted with Heidi Klum*

CORRELATION BETWEEN INCIDENCE OF GASTROENTERITIS AND HOCKEY ENTHUSIASM IN NORTH AMERICA

Incidence of Gastroenteritis

Incidence of Hockey

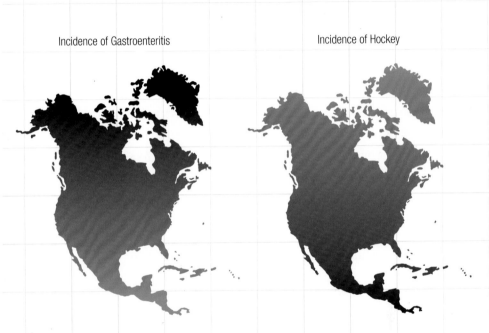

CONCLUSION: HOCKEY PREVENTS FOOD POISONING

| Low | Low–Mid | Common | Frequent |

Sources: Centers for Disease Control and Prevention, alexa.com, Google Trends

Space Travel

For decades, America was at the forefront of the space race. However, after the recent economic downturns, NASA has proven an easy target for budget cuts. As the United States has lost the will for space travel, rival powers like China as well as private citizens such as Richard Branson have taken up the mission of developing new space technologies. As our natural resources on earth dwindle and the number of environmental catastrophes increases, in seems inevitable that human beings will either all die out quite suddenly (McCarthy 2006), or we will return our interest to the mission of colonizing other planets before humanity becomes extinct.

In order to help the future decision makers of humanity's space migration (who may be reading this book even now, or may be reading it in a postapocalyptic bunker), we have provided this handy chart to forewarn future space travelers what manner of hazards to be prepared for on each planet in our solar system. We don't necessarily have solutions for these nine different flavors of certain doom, but perhaps knowing what to look out for will offer some advantage to the space refugees of tomorrow.

LEADING CAUSES OF DEATH
A PLANETARY GUIDE

Neptune

Pluto

Saturn

Cause of Death:
BURIED ALIVE

Reason:
LACK OF SOLID GROUND

Cause of Death:
TORN APART

Reason:
CONSTANT 1500 MPH WINDS

Cause of Death:
EMBARRASSMENT

Reason:
NOT A REAL PLANET

Cause of Death:
HEART DISEASE

Reason:
UBIQUITOUS FAST FOOD

Cause of Death:
HYPOXIA

Reason:
LACK OF ATMOSPHERE

Cause of Death:
HYPOTHERMIA

Reason:
AVERAGE SUMMER TEMP: -370°F

Earth

Mars

Uranus

Cause of Death:
IMMOLATION

Reason:
TOO CLOSE TO THE SUN

Cause of Death:
SUFFOCATION

Reason:
SULFURIC ACID ATMOSPHERE

Cause of Death:
CRUSHED TO DEATH

Reason:
INTENSE GRAVITY

Mercury

Venus

Jupiter

37

DOOMED CITIES OF THE U.S.

BIG SKY, MONTANA:
Proximity to Yellowstone Caldera

DOOM:
Exploded by super-volcano eruption

CHICAGO, ILLINOIS:
More nuclear reactors than any other state

DOOM:
Crushed by giant irradiated lizard

DETROIT, MICHIGAN:
Epicenter of collapsed American automobile industry

DOOM:
De-evolution into postapocalyptic hellscape

GUTTENBERG, NEW JERSEY:
Highest population density in the country

DOOM:
Decimated by communicable disease

LOS ANGELES, CALIFORNIA:
Built on San Andreas fault

DOOM:
Gigantic earthquake will drop the city into the ocean

MEMPHIS, TENNESSEE:
One of the most sedentary and obese cities in the world

DOOM:
Population unable to fit out front door

NEW ORLEANS, LOUISIANA:
Built below sea level

DOOM:
Consumed by ocean

WASHINGTON, D.C.:
Too many national monuments

DOOM:
Blown up during a montage by alien spaceships

Gender, Social Stratification, and Why Online Dating Blows

WHAT YOUR DRINK ORDER SAYS TO YOUR DATE

BEER
I will be fat someday.

MARTINI
I'm trying to keep things classy but also get wasted.

WINE
I'm trying to keep things classy.

RUM & COLA
I just turned 21.

ICED TEA
I will not sleep with you.

SHOTS
I will do anything tonight.

VODKA & ENERGY DRINK
I will do anything ALL night.

Real Drinks You Should Never Order

"To alcohol! The cause of, and solution to, all of life's problems."
—Homer J. Simpson

When those of us who aren't chemists say "alcohol," we are most likely referring to ethanol (C_2H_5OH), the simple acyclic alcohol found in alcoholic beverages, or "booze." Booze can be broken into three basic categories: beer, wine, and spirits. Beer is the oldest form of booze, and it is currently the third-most consumed beverage on the planet (after water and tea). Booze serves many practical social functions, from religious rituals to allowing unattractive people to briefly couple with attractive people. There have been very few cultures in human history that did not partake in boozing, and historians tend to agree that these groups were totally uncool and full of square buzzkills (Ramon 1982).

We currently live in a golden age of booze consumption, with varieties of alcohol and mixers from around the world easily acquirable at the local corner store. This has offered boozers and bartenders the chance to create a cornucopia of mixed-drink permutations, from timeless classics like the old-fashioned or the gimlet, to more modern inventions like the Sex on the Beach or the Appletini.

For every great invention, there are sure to be many far more terrible ones. Here are some mixed drinks you may want to steer clear of.

Real Drinks You Should <u>Never</u> Order for Your Date

Horse Jizz
~~~~~~~
1 part beer
1 part milk

Time of the Month
~~~~~~~
tomato juice
Wild Turkey

Cat Sick
~~~~~~~
1 part Kahlúa
1 part Bailey's
1 part brandy

Pap Smear
~~~~~~~
1 part Pabst Blue Ribbon
1 part Smirnoff
(dash of bitters optional)

Smoker's Cough
~~~~~~~
1 part Kahlúa
1 part Bailey's
1 part brandy

Lewinsky
~~~~~~~
1 part Bailey's
1 part SoCo
1 part peppermint schnapps

Salty Chihauhua
~~~~~~~
tequila
grapefruit juice
dash of salt

Brain Tumor
~~~~~~~
peach schnapps
Bailey's
cherry brandy
dash of grenadine

Bloody Tampon
~~~~~~~
1 part whiskey
1 part tequila
1 part vodka
V8
lemon juice
Bailey's

Drew Barrymore
~~~~~~~
Shirley Temple
vanilla vodka

43

Online Dating

Like it or not, online dating has become a key part of the modern dating scene. Some dating sites match you with potential mates through the use of a scientifically rigorous personality profiling test, while others use less scientific evaluations such as "Which Harry Potter character are you?" But ultimately, for 84 percent of the online dating population, the most important part of a profile is the pictures. While pictures are worth a thousand words, pictures often lie. Be on the lookout for:

1. Obvious signs of Photoshopping (user is fighting chronic acne)
2. Pictures taken from a high angle (user has fat thighs)
3. Pictures of lesser-known movie stars (user is actually a 70-year-old man)
4. People who never open their mouth when they smile (user has bad teeth)
5. Pictures of a sexy body with no head (user is possibly headless)

These are all signs that the person you're looking at is significantly less attractive than their profile indicates (Bradbey 2009).

WHAT ONLINE DATING BODY TYPES REALLY MEAN

RATHER NOT SAY

Fat

FIT

Fit

CURVY

Fat with big ass

THIN

Thin

AVERAGE

Fat

OVERWEIGHT

Orca fat

SKINNY

Thin but out of shape

JACKED

Too fit

USED UP

Thin but addicted to heroin

ATHLETIC

Fit but kinda fat

FULL-FIGURED

Fat with big boobs

A LITTLE EXTRA

Fat

45

Sleeping arrangements

Cold Night

Hot Night

Stormy Night

Fight Night

Women

Often looked at but little understood, women are the female version of men (Page and Shapiro 1927). They have many similar qualities (two arms, two legs), but also many differences (internal sexual organs, less offensive odor). Men are often heard complaining that they don't understand women, while just as often women seem to not understand themselves—studies indicate that up to 85 percent of women wear the wrong bra size (Scurr 2011).

How can we better understand this oft-misunderstood half of humanity? If only there were a series of charts laying out all you need to know! Oh wait, there is, on the following pages.

WHAT'S IN YOUR PURSE?

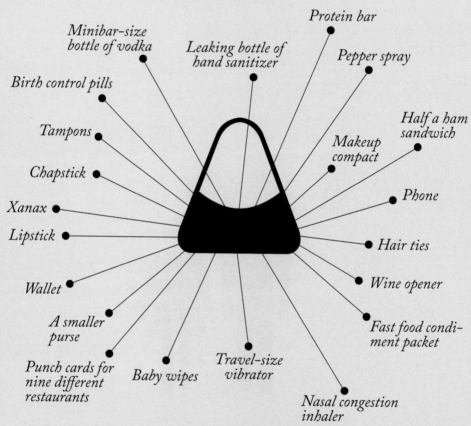

Minibar-size bottle of vodka

Leaking bottle of hand sanitizer

Protein bar

Pepper spray

Birth control pills

Tampons

Chapstick

Xanax

Lipstick

Makeup compact

Half a ham sandwich

Phone

Hair ties

Wallet

Wine opener

A smaller purse

Punch cards for nine different restaurants

Baby wipes

Travel-size vibrator

Fast food condiment packet

Nasal congestion inhaler

HOW TO TELL IF YOU'RE KNOCKED UP
(WITHOUT A PREGNANCY TEST)

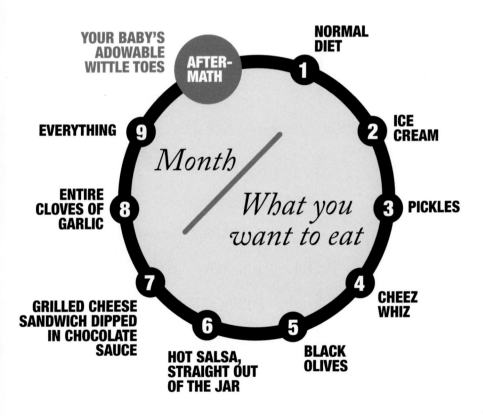

YOUR BABY'S ADOWABLE WITTLE TOES

AFTER-MATH

NORMAL DIET

1

EVERYTHING — 9

2 — ICE CREAM

Month

ENTIRE CLOVES OF GARLIC — 8

What you want to eat

3 — PICKLES

7

4 — CHEEZ WHIZ

GRILLED CHEESE SANDWICH DIPPED IN CHOCOLATE SAUCE

6

5

HOT SALSA, STRAIGHT OUT OF THE JAR

BLACK OLIVES

Amount of Skin Shown in Women's Fashion

Lots of Skin!

THE FUTURE / *Pasties*

1970s / *Short shorts*

1960s / *Miniskirt*

2000s / *Booty shorts/American apparel*

1920s / *Flapper dress*

1980s / *Leg warmers*

1940s / *Knee-length skirt*

1950s / *Poodle skirt*

1930s / *Wrap dress*

1910s / *Tunic*

1990s / *Baggy jeans*

Extremely Modest

WEDDING DATE CHECKLIST

Bride-to-be:

TO HIRE:

○ Chef
○ Band
○ Minister you're comfortable with

TO PLAN/PICK:

○ Wedding venue
○ Menu
○ Floral arrangements
○ Gift registry
○ Bridesmaid dresses
○ Groomsman tuxes
○ Wedding dress
○ Honeymoon

TO SEND/RECEIVE:

○ "Save the dates"
○ Invitations
○ RSVPs

TO SCHEDULE:

○ Diet
○ Panic attack

Groom-to-be:

TO DO:

○ Anything you're told to do

Men

Men are the male versions of *Homo sapiens*, easily distinguished from women by their slightly larger size, profuse body hair, and nonmatching clothing. While the female mind perplexes men with its enigmatic complexity, the male mind similarly perplexes women with its unsophisticated simplicity. Easily placated and manipulated by breasts and food, men initially rose as the dominant of the two sexes through aggressive tendencies and the ability to urinate while standing up. This led to men "planting their flag," so to speak, in a lot of important areas, like using their name in words such as *human*, *mankind*, and *manatee*. But man has been slipping from his pedestal ever since.

Women tend to feel as though they cannot figure out the men in their lives, when the likely reality is that these men are just dumb. And no one is better at being dumb than men. So let us revel in the simplistic glory of male maleness.

REASON YOU WENT FISHING TODAY

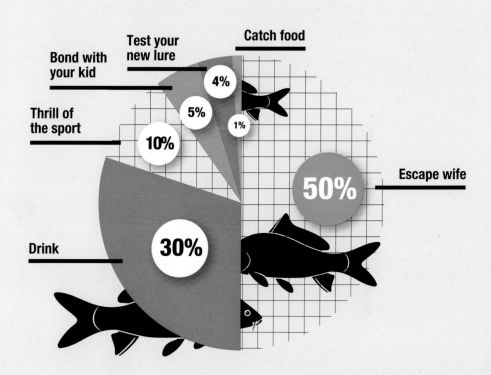

Bond with your kid

Test your new lure

Catch food

Thrill of the sport

Escape wife

Drink

4%

5%

1%

10%

50%

30%

WHAT'S IN YOUR WALLET?

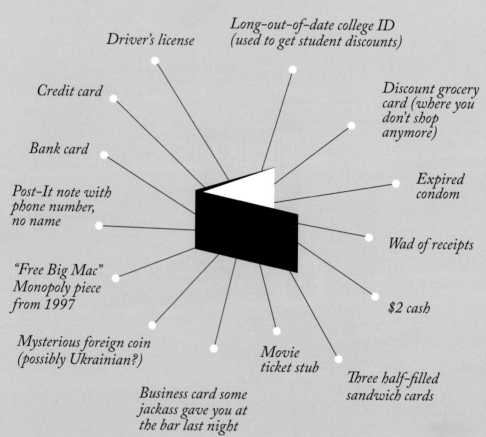

Driver's license

Long-out-of-date college ID (used to get student discounts)

Credit card

Discount grocery card (where you don't shop anymore)

Bank card

Expired condom

Post-It note with phone number, no name

Wad of receipts

"Free Big Mac" Monopoly piece from 1997

$2 cash

Mysterious foreign coin (possibly Ukrainian?)

Movie ticket stub

Three half-filled sandwich cards

Business card some jackass gave you at the bar last night

AXLE ROWS

	NUMBER OF WHEELS	IF YOU DRIVE IT YOU ARE A…	WHAT DO YOU DO WHILE DRIVING?	WEAKNESS
UNICYCLE	1	Clown	Juggle	Gravity
MOTORCYCLE	2	Badass	Piss off people in cars	Open car doors
TRICYCLE	3	Toddler	Honk your toy horn	Loose gravel
CAR	4	Adult	Text	Bird poop
6-WHEELER ATV	6	Redneck	Drink beer	Sudden trees
ARMORED MILITARY VEHICLE	8	Soldier	Watch for IEDs	Armor-piercing bullets
BIG-RIG TRUCK	18	Trucker	Talk on the CB radio	Trucker tan

Beards

On the sixth day of creation, God created "man." Roughly 13 to 15 years later, hairs began sprouting out of that man's face, most likely first making themselves noticed as embarrassing fuzz on his upper lip (Darwin 1871). From that point forward, beards became an integral part of male identity. In the ancient world, great care was paid toward how a beard was worn. Mesopotamian men oiled their beards, and the Egyptian pharaohs so thoroughly believed that a kickass goatee was a sign of sovereignty that queens often wore false beards.

Then, just as men were really getting into their beards, the Macedonians came along and ruined everything by introducing the clean-shaven look. Alexander the Great not only put his baby-smooth visage on coins and statues around the world, he demanded that all his soldiers be cleanly shaved as well, fearing that beards presented an obvious battlefield disadvantage. And, thus, man's daily war with razor burn began.

Since those days, malekind has waged an unending battle to not shave, often losing to fashion trends and disapproving girlfriends and wives.

To Beard or Not to Beard?

PROS

CONS

PROS		CONS
No shaving = Time saved	↔	Look older and fatter
Ugly? Beard will hide your hideous face	↔	Attractive? Beard will hide your handsome face
Defense from the elements	↔	Magnet for food
Some ladies dig it	↔	Most ladies don't
You'll look more like Zach Galifianakis	↔	You'll look more like Zach Galifianakis
Less aerodynamic when running	↔	More wind resistance when falling from a cliff
A lot of famous intellectuals had beards	↔	So did a lot of crazy maniacs and murderers

PHILOSOPHICAL FACIAL HAIR

JEAN PAUL SARTRE
*"A lost battle is a battle
one thinks one has lost."*

MARTIN HEIDEGGER
*"The possible ranks higher
than the actual."*

RENÉ DESCARTES
"I think, therefore I am."

ARTHUR
SCHOPENHAUER
*"A man can be himself only
so long as he is alone."*

FRIEDRICH NIETZSCHE
*"Ah, women. They make the
highs higher and the lows
more frequent."*

HENRY DAVID THOREAU
*"Be not simply good—be good
for something."*

EDMUND HUSSERL
*"Experience by itself is
not science"*

SOCRATES
*"He is richest who is content
with the least, for content is
the wealth of nature. "*

KARL MARX
*"From each according
to his abilities, to each
according to his needs."*

{ SUPER FANS! }

	MUSIC	SPORTS	SCI-FI/FANTASY	RELIGION	TECH-NOLOGY
COMMNONLY MISTAKEN AS	Aficionados	Men	Geniuses	Family-oriented	Savvy
ACTUALLY	Groupies	Boys	Nerds	Irrational zealots	Geeks
COMMONLY FOUND AT	Coachella, SXSW	A couch	Comic-Con	Church	Apple stores
SPOT THEM WEARING	Concert Ts	Replica jerseys	Pointy ears	Modest clothing	Ironic Nintendo shirts
SEX REQUIRES	Backstage passes	An off-season	Costumes	Massive cover-ups, therapy	Vibrators
EMBARRASSING SIDE EFFECT	STDs	Body paint	Protracted virginity	Funeral protests	Credit-card-related bankruptcy

SOCIAL STRATIFICATION OF THE SOCIALLY CHALLENGED

Nerd

Technical description:
Book smart, socially awkward

Celebrity example:
Mark Zuckerberg

Hobbies:
Hacking

Classic accessory:
Pocket protector

What kind of party would they throw?
Astronomy club party

Geek

Technical description:
Obsessed with uncool things

Celebrity example:
Harry Knowles

Hobbies:
Sci-fi TV show marathons

Classic accessory:
Dr. Who T-shirt

What kind of party would they throw?
Cosplay party

Dork

Technical description:
A nerd who isn't smart

Celebrity example:
Tucker Carlson

Hobbies:
Talking about how smart they are

Classic accessory:
Bow tie

What kind of party would they throw?
Board game night

Spaz

Technical description:
Embarrassingly excitable

Celebrity example:
Kanye West

Hobbies:
Switching hobbies

Classic accessory:
Ritalin

What kind of party would they throw?
Dance party

Loser

Technical description:
Self-inflicted friendlessness

Celebrity example:
Lindsay Lohan

Hobbies:
Complaining about how persecuted they are

Classic accessory:
Bad attitude

What kind of party would they throw?
Pity party

Tool

Technical description:
Confidence disproportional to likability

Celebrity example:
The Situation

Hobbies:
Lying about sexual exploits

Classic accessory:
Fake tan

What kind of party would they throw?
Orgy

Compiled Life Advice from Two Single Scientists

WORLD LAW ENFORCEMENT

YOU ARE DRUNK AND DISORDERLY. WHAT YOU SHOULD EXPECT FROM AN APPROACHING POLICE OFFICER:

ITALY
Aggressively hit on you.

U.S.
Accidentally "taze" you with their handgun.

U.K.
Beat you with billy clubs.

MEXICO
Patiently wait for a bribe.

RUSSIA
Secrete you away to Mafia organ-harvesting dungeon.

CANADA
Politely ask you to stop.

FRANCE
Turn up their noses at you in disdain.

IRELAND
Drink you into submission.

The Modern Ten Commandments

I
Thou shall have no other gods.
For God is insecure and has
trust issues.

II
Thou shall not make for yourself
any graven idols save thou find
the face of Jesus in your toast.

III
Thou shall not take the name of
the Lord your God in vain;
"Holy Shit" is preferable.

IV
Remember the Sabbath day, for
football shall be on all day.

V
Honor thy father and mother
by accepting their Facebook
friend requests.

VI
Thou shall not murder outside
of video games.

VII
Thou shall not "sext"
adulterously, for it is
still cheating.

VIII
Thou shall not BitTorrent
or file share.

IX
Thou shall not cyber bully
thy neighbor.

X
Thou shall not covet thy
neighbor's ass; purchase thine
own Spanx.

WHAT TO DO IF YOU BREAK YOUR WRIST

You broke your wrist Saturday morning playing football. **Don't panic.** Just follow these simple steps.

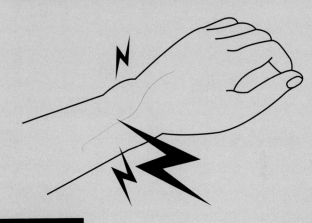

STEP 1
Use a magazine and rubber bands to stabilize arm.

STEP 2
Keep wrist iced to reduce swelling.

STEP 3
Relax. Power through the pain until Monday.

STEP 4
Go to work and pretend to break your wrist.

STEP 5
Get medical treatment and worker's comp.

65

THE *Highs* AND *Lows* OF AGING PRIVILEGES

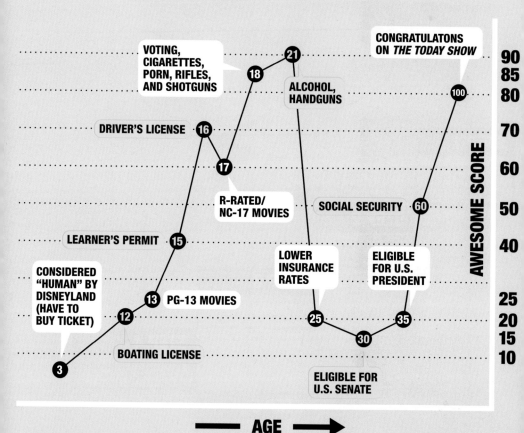

WHAT FACE TATTOO IS APPROPRIATE FOR ME?

Are you (a)...?	Tattoo of choice	Significance
Maori native of New Zealand	Intricate spirals	Your social status
Roman slave	Text that reads "Stop me, I'm a runaway"	To discourage your escape
Prison gangster	A teardrop	You have killed someone
Mike Tyson	Pacific Islander-esque tribal design	You're Mike Tyson
Housewife of Orange County	Permanent lip liner	Time saver!
Frat boy	Penis and testicles (permanence optional)	You passed out drunk
Hipster	Fake mustache under your real mustache	Ironic
Punk girl	Star pattern	Daddy issues

The Smoker's Twelve-Step Program

1 SMOKE A PACK A DAY
2 DECIDE TO QUIT SMOKING
3 TRY COLD TURKEY
4 BUY A CARTON
5 BUY NICOTINE GUM (AND ANOTHER PACK CIGARETTES)
6 BUY THE PATCH AND NICOTINE GUM (AND ANOTHER PACK)
7 FIND SOME NEW INNER RESOLVE
8 QUIT. BECOME AN EMOTIONAL WRECK
9 SUCCESS! YOU'RE A NONSMOKER
10 CELEBRATE!
11 GET DRUNK, HAVE JUST ONE CIGARETTE
12 RETURN TO STEP ONE

PARENT'S GUIDE TO HOLIDAYS

HOLIDAY	CHRISTMAS	NEW YEAR'S EVE	VALENTINE'S DAY	PRESIDENT'S DAY	EASTER	JULY 4TH	HALLOWEEN	THANKSGIVING
CELE-BRATING	Jesus	The new year	Love	The U.S. government	Jesus	U.S.	Pagans	Indians and Pilgrims
MASCOT	Santa Claus	Dick Clark	Cupid	George Washington	Egg-laying bunny	Uncle Sam	Pumpkins	Turkey
FOR KIDS IT MEANS	Getting presents!	Staying up late	Valentines from the entire class	No school	Candy	Fireworks	Candy and costumes	Forced to play with relatives
FOR ADULTS IT MEANS	Buying presents	Getting drunk before midnight	Getting drunk alone/with your mate	Buying mattresses	Hiding eggs	Getting drunk at barbecues	Getting drunk, in costume	Falling asleep after dinner, drunk

WHY YOU GO TO THE BATHROOM DURING WORK

15%
To use bathroom

85%
Excuse to not work

BOWLING IMPAIRMENT CHART

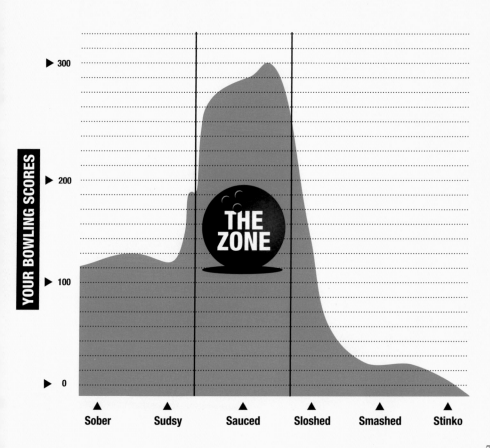

The Fork and the Chopstick

FORK:

Common adoption: c. AD 1600

Variations: Salad, dessert, fondue, dinner, serving, carving, spork, sporf

Materials: Metal, plastic

Best used with: Spaghetti

Greatest strength: Easy to use

Greatest failing: Soup

Secret benefit: Commonly used weapon

Secret drawback: Sits on the left side of the plate but you use it with your right hand

CHOPSTICK:

Common adoption: c.1200 BC

Variations: Long (cooking/frying), short (eating), tapered, pointy, blunt, deadly

Materials: Bamboo, plastic, wood, bone, metal, jade, ivory

Best used with: Sushi

Greatest strength: Versatile grasping sizes

Greatest failing: Ironically, rice

Secret benefit: Exercises your brain, decreasing senility

Secret drawback: May slightly increase the risk of osteoarthritis in hand

THE FIVE STAGES OF A HANGOVER AT WORK

Physical and Emotional Well-Being

"Oh crap, I'm so hungover. What did I do?"

Bargaining
1:30 p.m.

Shitty

"For the love of . . . I swear, I'll never drink again. Just make the pain go away."

Anger
10:30 a.m.

Awesome

Depression
3:30 p.m.

Denial
8:00 a.m.

Dying

"I'm such an idiot. I should be fired for this. Someone kill me."

"I'm not that hungover. I just need water."

Acceptance
5:00 p.m.

"This isn't so bad. I've made it! I'll survive! Oh hey, it's almost happy hour . . ."

SHOULD I BE DRINKING?
Alcoholic's Cheat Sheet

OKAY TO GET DRUNK

Your birthday

A wedding

Bachelor party

At a bar

Boating

Reading a novel

Watching boxing

Taking a plane

Fat Tuesday

Lounging by the pool

NOT OKAY TO GET DRUNK

A 10-year-old's birthday

A bris

Divorce hearing

Taking the bar

Driving

Reading a speeding ticket

Boxing

Piloting a plane

Good Friday

Scuba diving

Pet Owner's Cheat Sheet

CAT

- **You live in:** An apartment
- **Upside:** Cuddles!
- **Downside:** Allergies
- **How your pet feels about you:** Toleration in exchange for food
- **Equivalent of:** Passive-aggressive roommate

DOG

- **You live in:** A house
- **Upside:** Pick up dates
- **Downside:** Pick up poop
- **How your pet feels about you:** Undying love and devotion
- **Equivalent of:** Lovesick stalker

BIRD

- **You live in:** A nursing home
- **Upside:** Chirping
- **Downside:** Chirping
- **How your pet feels about you:** You're a warden.
- **Equivalent of:** Noise machine that shits

SNAKE

- **You live in:** Your parents' basement
- **Upside:** Watching it eat
- **Downside:** You own a snake.
- **How your pet feels about you:** Waiting for you to die. To eat you.
- **Equivalent of:** Badass living ninja sword

RABBIT

- **You live in:** The boonies
- **Upside:** Infinite supply of offspring
- **Downside:** Infinite supply of tiny poop. Everywhere.
- **How your pet feels about you:** Your shoelaces look delicious.
- **Equivalent of:** Giant hamster

FISH

- **You live in:** A professionally decorated home
- **Upside:** Ambience
- **Downside:** Random floating corpses
- **How your pet feels about you:** Terrified
- **Equivalent of:** Painting that must be continuously cleaned

Pet Calculus

People have always liked having pets. Initially, our animal companions served a more utilitarian purpose. Dogs were the first wild species to be domesticated by humans, when our Stone Age ancestors used the increasingly tame offspring of wolves to aid in hunting and security some 15,000 years ago (Savolainen et al. 2002). Cats indifferently entered our lives roughly 9,000 years ago to help rid our homes of pesky rodents (Driscoll, MacDonald, and O'Brien 2009). But even back then we surely delighted in the site of a sleepy kitten or a dog chasing its own tail.

Very few modern Americans acquire a pet for such specific tasks. The enjoyment and low-level entertainment their antics provide us—and millions of daily YouTube viewers—have become their chief appeal. They are simply an integral and familiar aspect of our lives. Of course, as they say, familiarity breeds contempt. Pets, like people, can be annoying, too, and there are a few universal and irksome truths about our beloved animal companions that we have laid out for you using the infallibility of math.

PET CALCULUS

Number of times your dog poops during a walk = {Y}

Number of plastic bags you're carrying = {X}

Then: {Y = X + 1}

Your desire to pet your cat = {X}

Your cat's desire to be petted = {Y}

Then: $\{X = \dfrac{1}{Y}\}$

Your girlfriend's pet's lifespan = {X years}

Your hatred of that pet on a scale of 1 to 10 = {Y}

Then: {X = Y x 2}

MOST EXTREME

SPORTS SIDE EFFECTS

SKYDIVING: Death

BALLET: Psychotic break with reality

BULLFIGHTING: Groin loss

FOOTBALL: Brain loss

BOXING: Facial disfigurement

HOCKEY: Tooth loss

BASKETBALL: Knee pain

GOLF: Lower-back strain

COMPETITIVE EATING: Heartburn

POKER: Paper cuts

SHUFFLEBOARD: Arthritis-related discomfort

CHESS: Headaches/irritability

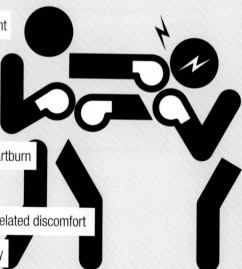

LEAST EXTREME

HOW MUCH ESPRESSO?

8 SHOTS: GRAND MAL SEIZURE/BINGO

7 SHOTS: HEART PALPITATIONS

6 SHOTS: PERCEPTION OF EXTRA MENTAL POWERS

5 SHOTS: SHAKY HANDS

4 SHOTS: HYPERAWARE

3 SHOTS: ALERT

2 SHOTS: SEMIFUNCTIONAL

1 SHOT: ASLEEP

Farting: An Existential Dilemma

Believe it or not, for all its uncouth silliness, the word *fart* is one of the oldest in the English language. It derives from the Middle English words *ferten* or *farten*, which themselves came from the Old High German word for breaking wind, *ferzan* (Hughes 2000).

Despite its negative reputation, farting is nonetheless an ordinary and inescapable bodily function. While it is typically considered humorous among males, particularly children—who may partake in "Dutch ovening" and "wafting"—farting is deemed rude in public or

 mixed company. Most of us attempt to release our farts into the world as discretely as possible. Alas, sometimes one has eaten Indian food or a particularly spicy burrito, and the fart just sneaks out on its own, with no permission from the farter. It's a situation that can prove embarrassing.

Luckily, we have provided the following flowchart, which will guide you away from catastrophe and optimize the outcomes of your accidental anal emissions.

Hot Air Head-Scratcher

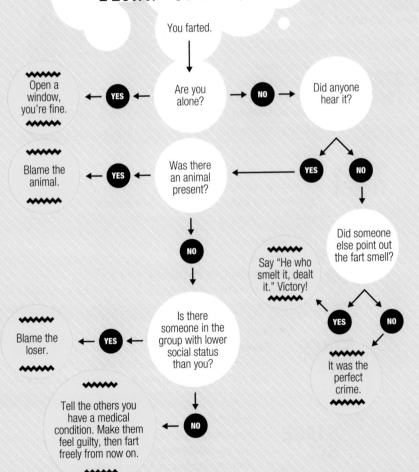

You farted.

Are you alone?

YES → Open a window, you're fine.

NO → Did anyone hear it?

YES → Was there an animal present?

YES → Blame the animal.

NO → Is there someone in the group with lower social status than you?

YES → Blame the loser.

NO → Tell the others you have a medical condition. Make them feel guilty, then fart freely from now on.

NO → Did someone else point out the fart smell?

YES → Say "He who smelt it, dealt it." Victory!

NO → It was the perfect crime.

STAGE ONE
(JUST LAID OFF)

Mood: Relaxed, happy
Financial situation: Flush and living the dream
How you spend your day: Yoga, sleeping
Jobs you're looking at: Not really looking

THE SIX STAGES OF UNEMPLOYMENT

STAGE TWO

Mood: Earnest
Financial situation: Savings are dwindling
How you spend your day: Daytime TV
Jobs you're looking at: Only jobs that are better than your previous one

STAGE THREE

Mood: Anxious
Financial situation: Serious
How you spend your day: Craigslist
Jobs you're looking at: Any kind of job that pays okay

STAGE FOUR

Mood: Concerned
Financial situation: Dire
How you spend your day: Day-long panic attacks
Jobs you're looking at: Demeaning jobs similar to what you did as a teenager

STAGE FIVE

Mood: Panicked
Financial situation: Broke
How you spend your day: Sleep all day. Stay up all night.
Jobs you're looking at: Anything. You will train to be a migrant worker.

STAGE SIX

Mood: Overjoyed
Financial situation: Turns out you get an extension on your unemployment!
How you spend your day: Partying
Jobs you're looking at: Who needs a job, man?

The Pros and Cons of a Pros-and-Cons List

PRO

CON

PRO	CON
HELPS VISUALIZE YOUR PROBLEM.	ULTIMATELY CONFUSING.
YOU LOOK ORGANIZED.	YOU LOOK LIKE YOU HAVE OCD.
YOU'RE ACCOMPLISHING SOMETHING!	LIST-MAKING IS ANOTHER FORM OF PROCRASTINATION.
IMPRESS YOUR SIGNIFICANT OTHER WITH INITIATIVE!	IS YOUR LIST TITLED *SHOULD WE STAY TOGETHER?* LESS IMPRESSIVE.
YOU CAN ADD UP THE PROS AND CONS AND JUST GO WITH WHICHEVER HAS THE MOST.	NOT EVERY *PRO* OR *CON* IS EQUALLY IMPORTANT, IDIOT.
IF YOU GET AMNESIA, YOU'LL STILL KNOW JUST WHERE YOU WERE IN THE DECISION-MAKING PROCESS.	IT WOULD BE EASIER FOR FUTURE AMNESIAC YOU IF YOU'D JUST MADE A DECISION ALREADY.
YOUR MOTHER SAYS SHE ALWAYS MAKES *PROS AND CONS* LISTS.	YOU ARE TURNING INTO YOUR MOTHER.

PROTECTIVE, LIFE-SAVING GEAR

SPACE SUIT – *OUTER SPACE*

SUIT OF ARMOR – *MEDIEVAL EUROPE*

HAZMAT SUIT – *TOXIC WASTE DUMP*

LEATHER GIMP SUIT – *S&M ORGY*

GORE-TEX SNOWSUIT – *MINNESOTA*

SCUBA GEAR – *UNDERWATER*

METAL STAR WARS BIKINI – *COMIC-CON*

The Sandwich
and the Semicolon

Homeland Security
Threat Levels: 1776

Severe

(incarnadine)
British approach imminent.
Arm women, children, slaves.
Break out pointy hats.

Elevated

(tangerine)
Prepare emergency kits.
Medical supplies: saw, leeches,
Bibles. Sustenance: hardtack,
salted cod, tobacco. Begin
loading muskets.

High

(daffodil)
Conserve whale oil by
extinguishing lanterns.
Prepare muskets for firing.
Steel patriotic constitutions.

Guarded

(navy)
Should British soldiers
demand quartering in your
house, pretend you are not
home. Be alert for breaking
news pamphlets.

Low

(olive)
Take time to learn to read.
Prepare disaster plan with
family/faithful indentured
servants.

FAMOUS
Caesars & Cesars
PART I

	JULIUS CAESAR	BLACK CAESAR	CAESAR SALAD
WHO	An Emperor	A Gangster	A Salad
COMMANDS	The Roman Empire	Harlem	Light Dinner Fare
ENEMY	Democracy	The Man	American Obesity
KNOWN FOR	Crossing the Rubicon	Straight Razors to Enemy Ears	Tasting Awesome
OVER-SHADOWED BY	Augustus	Shaft	Taco Salads
WORST SIDE	Ushering in Hundreds of Years of Dictatorship	Rape and Murder	Salmonella Poisoning

FAMOUS
Caesars & Cesars
PART II

	CESAR CHAVEZ	**CESAR ROMERO**	**CESAR MILLAN**
WHO	A Labor Leader	An Actor	The Dog Whisperer
COMMANDS	United Farm Workers	1960s Gotham Underwold	Poorly Trained Canines
ENEMY	Exploitative Employers	Batman	Misbehavior
KNOWN FOR	Hunger Strikes	Laughing Gas	Being the "Pack Leader"
OVER-SHADOWED BY	Gandhi	Jack Nicholson, Heath Ledger	Super Nanny and Gordon Ramsay
QUOTE	"In some cases, nonviolence requires more militancy than violence."	"I can't date women my own age anymore—I hate going to cemeteries."	"I rehabilitate dogs. I train people."

A BREAKDOWN OF FAMOUS REVOLUTIONS

4.5 Billion Years BC

EARTH'S REVOLUTION

➡ **Lasted:** 365.25 days (continuing)

⭐ **Benefited:** Life

⬇ **Loser:** Ptolemaic model

⬆ **Winner:** Physics

Late 18th Century

AMERICAN REVOLUTION

➡ **Lasted:** 1777–1783

⭐ **Benefited:** Colonialists

⬇ **Loser:** British

⬆ **Winner:** U.S.

Mid-20th Century

SEXUAL REVOLUTION

➡ **Lasted:** 1960s–1980s

⭐ **Benefited:** Sex addicts

⬇ **Loser:** Squares

⬆ **Winner:** STDs

Early 21st Century

DANCE DANCE REVOLUTION

➡ **Lasted:** 1998–present

⭐ **Benefited:** Arcade owners

⬇ **Loser:** Obese Americans

⬆ **Winner:** Asian teens

NAMESAKE THINGS

What it could have been called:
THE FOOD STACK

THE SANDWICH

Inventor:
John Mantagu,
the 4th Earl of
Sandwich

SHRAPNEL

What it could have been called:
BLASTY BITS

Inventor:
Major General Henry
Shrapnel

THE SOUSAPHONE

What it could have been called:
THE WRAP-AROUND TUBA

Inventor:
John Philip Sousa

THE LEOTARD

What it could have been called:
THE LEGLESS BODY GLOVE

Inventor:
Jules Leotard

GRANNY SMITH APPLE

What it could have been called:
A GREEN APPLE

Inventor:
Maria Ann
"Granny" Smith

BRAILLE

What it could have been called:
BLIND BUMPS

Inventor:
Louis Braille

THE CARDIGAN

What it could have been called:
THE OPEN-FACE SWEATER

Inventor:
James Brudenell,
the 7th Earl of
Cardigan

THE UZI

What it could have been called:
THE MIDGET'S MACHINE GUN

Inventor:
Uziel Gal

MAU-SOLEUM

What it could have been called:
CORPSE HUT

Inventor:
Mausolus

THE GUILLOTINE

What it could have been called:
THE HEAD RE-MOVER

Inventor:
Joseph-Ignace
Guillotin

GORE-TEX

What it could have been called:
BREATHABLE POLYTET-RAFLUO-ROTH-YLENE

Inventor:
Bill Gore

O CAPTAIN! MY CAPTAIN!

CAPTAIN COOK

Commander of:
HMS *Endeavour*

Achievement:
Discovered Hawaii

Downfall:
Killed by Hawaiians

CAP'N CRUNCH

Commander of:
Breakfast

Achievement:
Discovered Crunch Berries

Downfall:
Sogginess

CAPTAIN NEMO

Commander of:
The *Nautilus*

Achievement:
Defeated a giant squid

Downfall:
Lost his entire crew in a storm

CAPTAIN MORGAN

Commander of:
Spring Break

Achievement:
Discovered rum and cola

Downfall: Diabetes

CAPTAIN KIRK

Commander of:
USS *Enterprise*

Achievement:
Defeated Kahn

Downfall:
Botched Priceline negotiation

★★★★★★★ POLITICAL PARTIES ★★★★★★★	★★★★★★★ REPUBLICANS ★★★★★★★	★★★★★★★ DEMOCRATS ★★★★★★★	★★★★★★★ THIRD PARTIES ★★★★★★★
PROUD OF	Abraham Lincoln, Ronald Reagan	Franklin Roosevelt, John F. Kennedy	Jesse Ventura, Michael Bloomberg
ASHAMED OF	Richard Nixon	Jimmy Carter	Ross Perot
RESPONSIBLE FOR	Lower taxes on rich people	Civil rights	George W. Bush getting elected
VOTED FOR BY	White men	All other colors and genders	Hippies and survivalists
TYPICAL SCANDAL	Caught cheating on wife with a younger man	Caught cheating on wife with a younger woman	Caught cheating on favorite prostitute with a younger prostitute
WHAT THEY THINK OF EACH OTHER	Democrats are a bunch of mooching, Communist, pot-smoking Nazis	Republicans are a bunch of racist, exploitative, authoritarian Nazis	America's two-party system is bullcrap

Art History 101

In 1984, the art world was drastically and eternally changed when artists Kevin Eastman and Peter Laird created the *Teenage Mutant Ninja Turtles*. In their timeless story, a mutated rat named Splinter finds four baby turtles, who themselves become mutated. Splinter teaches them the ways of the Japanese art of ninjutsu, and, naturally, names them after four famous Renaissance artists. The characters became a worldwide sensation, and for all Americans born into the post–*Ninja Turtle* world, the names Leonardo, Donatello, Michelangelo, and Raphael no longer properly conjure up images of oil paints and celebrated frescoes. In the interest of both preserving the grand history of Italian art, as well as the nostalgic memory of our own Heroes in a Half Shell, we'd like to submit a combination of all eight individuals into an easy-to-remember amalgam for future education.

ART HISTORY 101:
FAMOUS ITALIAN PAINTERS
(FROM WHAT I REMEMBER)

Leonardo

Famous work: *The Mona Lisa*
Famous invention: The helicopter, tank
Taught by: Verrocchio
Primary role: He led.
Weapon of choice: Katana
Favorite food: Pizza

Raphael

Famous Work: *The School of Athens*
Famous invention: The alternate identity the "Nightwatcher"
Taught by: Pietro Perugino
Primary role: He was cool but crude.
Weapon of choice: Sai
Favorite food: Pizza

Donatello

Famous work: The bronze *David*
Famous invention: Dimensional portal
Taught by: Splinter
Primary role: He did machines.
Weapon of choice: Bo staff
Favorite food: Pizza

Michelangelo

Famous work: The Sistine Chapel
Famous invention: The dome of St. Peter's
Taught by: Bertoldo di Giovanni
Primary role: He was a party dude.
Weapon of choice: Nunchucks
Favorite food: Pizza

American Editor's Manual of Style: Punctuation Guide

PUNCTUATION	SHORTENED "MARK"	USE IT WHEN. . .
PERIOD	.	SPEAKING OF A WOMAN'S MENSTRUAL CYCLE
COLON	:	REFERRING TO THE HUMAN LARGE INTESTINE
SEMICOLON	;	REFERRING TO THE HUMAN SMALL INTESTINE
BRACKET	{	FILLING OUT AN NCAA OFFICE POOL
DASH	—	REFERENCING A SHORT, QUICKLY RUN RACE
SLASH	/	DRAFTING A BIOGRAPHY OF GUNS N' ROSES
POUND	#	REFERENCING WEIGHT (U.S.) /ALTERNATIVE HANDSHAKES

TEN GREAT BOOKS
RUINED IN <u>ONE</u> SENTENCE

The Maltese Falcon / **FALCON IS A FAKE.**

The Da Vinci Code / **JESUS HAD KIDS.**

The Great Gatsby / **GATSBY GETS SHOT AND DIES.**

Murder on the Orient Express / **THEY ALL DID IT.**

The Old Man and the Sea / **SHARKS EAT THE FISH.**

Moby Dick / **THE WHALE WINS.**

The Hitchhiker's Guide to the Galaxy / **THE ANSWER IS 42.**

Ender's Game / **IT WASN'T A GAME.**

Animal Farm / **PIGS TURN INTO HUMANS.**

Where's Waldo? / **HE'S JUST TO THE LEFT AND LITTLE BIT UP.**

340 lb

HOWARD TAFT
(1857–1930)

Famous for:
Being the 27th president of the United States.

Fun fact:
After becoming stuck in the White House bathtub, he had a special plus-size tub installed.

350 lb

WILLIAM THE CONQUEROR
(1027–1078)

Famous for:
Conquered England for the Normans.

Fun fact:
When they tried to cram his too-fat corpse into his too-small sarcophagus, his body exploded. Historical records indicate it was really disgusting.

375 lb

ORSON WELLES
(1915–1985)

Famous for:
Directing *Citizen Kane*.

Fun fact:
Had to go on a diet to play the famously fat Sir John Falstaff in *Chimes at Midnight*.

ROUND PEOPLE

382 lb

WILLIAM "THE REFRIGERATOR" PERRY
(1962–present)

Famous for:
Years as a Pro Bowl defensive lineman for the Chicago Bears.

Fun fact:
His Super Bowl ring size is 25; the average adult male ring size is 10–12.

580 lb

YAMAMOTOYAMA RYUTA
(1984–present)

Famous for:
Being the heaviest Japanese-born sumo wrestler ever.

Fun fact:
Once reportedly ate 146 pieces of sushi in a single meal.

757 lb

ISRAEL "IZ" KAMAKAWI WO`OLE
(1959–1997)

Famous for:
His ukulele medley of "Over the Rainbow" and "What a Wonderful World."

Fun fact:
The only nongovernment person to have their corpse lay in state in Honolulu's capital building.

1400 lb

JON BROWER MINNOCH
(1941–1983)

Famous for:
Holding the record for being the fattest man of all time.

Fun fact:
Once went on a diet and lost 920 pounds.

TALL PEOPLE

6'2"
JULIA CHILD
(1912–2004)

Famous for:
The French Chef

Fun fact:
Too tall for the Women's Army Corps, she joined the Office of Strategic Services (OSS) during WWII.

6'9"
ED "TOO TALL" JONES
(1951–present)

Famous for:
NFL defensive lineman

Fun fact:
Retired from football to box professionally, won every bout, retired from boxing, and played eight more years in the NFL.

8'11"
ROBERT WADLOW
(1918–1940)

Famous for:
Tallest man ever

Fun fact:
Twelve pallbearers were required to carry his 10-foot-long coffin at his funeral

6'9"
MICHAEL CRICHTON
(1942–2008)

Famous for:
Jurrasic Park

Fun fact:
Was a medical doctor, but came to believe that all ailments are caused by the patient's state of mind.

6'5"
ABRAHAM LINCOLN
(1809–1865)

Famous for:
U.S president

Fun fact:
Kept his important papers and letters inside the lining of his giant top hat.

7'2"
KEVIN PETER HALL
(1955–1991)

Famous for:
Predator

Fun fact:
His father was 6' 6", his mother 6' 2", and all his brothers were over 6'5".

7'7"
MANUTE BOL
(1962–2010)

Famous for:
NBA player

Fun fact:
Only NBA player to have more career blocked shots than points scored.

7'4"
ANDRE THE GIANT
(1946–1993)

Famous for:
Professional wrestler/ movie star

Fun fact:
Once drank 156 cans of beer in one sitting.

SMALL PEOPLE

HENRI DE TOLOUSE-LAUTREC
(1864–1901)

Famous for:
French post-impressionist painter

Fun fact:
Huge genitals.

5'1"

ALEXANDER POPE
(1688–1744)

Famous for:
Poet

Fun fact:
Third-most frequently quoted writer in *The Oxford Dictionary of Quotations*.

4'6"

BENITO JUAREZ
(1806–1872)

Famous for:
Five-time president of Mexico

Fun fact:
First full-blooded indigenious national ever to lead a country in the Western Hemisphere.

4'6"

MATILDA OF FLANDERS
(1031–1083)

Famous for:
Wife of William the Conqueror

Fun fact:
Literally beaten into marriage.

4'2"

JOE C
(1974–2000)

Famous for:
Kid Rock's sidekick

Fun fact:
Needed to take 60 pills a day for his various ailments.

3'9"

WEE MAN
(1973–present)

Famous for:
Jackass

Fun fact:
Can kick himself in the head.

4'

GENERAL TOM THUMB
(1834–1883)

Famous for:
Performing with P. T. Barnum

Fun fact:
Performed comedy for Queen Victoria and was a huge hit.

2'9"

WARWICK DAVIS
(1970–present)

Famous for:
Harry Potter

Fun fact:
Was only 12 when he played an ewok in *The Return of the Jedi*.

3'6"

PEOPLE WHO FAMOUSLY OVERCAME HANDICAPS

STEPHEN HAWKING | Developed amyotrophic lateral sclerosis in his early 20s → Became one of the greatest minds in theoretical physics and cosmology

MATT MURDOCK | Blinded by radioactive substance → Became the superhero Daredevil

CHRISTY BROWN | Born with cerebral palsy → Became an author, painter, and poet and wrote the autobiography *My Left Foot*

HELEN KELLER | Born deaf, dumb, and blind → Became a famous author and political activist

ERIK WEI-HENMAYER | Went completely blind by age 13 → Became a champion wrestler and marathon runner, and scaled Mount Everest

THOMAS DEMPSEY | Born with no toes on his right foot → Became an NFL kicker; holds the record for longest field goal

Stephen Baldwin, Optimus Prime, and Pop Culture Nuggets

THE OFFICIAL GUIDE TO CONANS

CONAN O'BRIEN

CONAN THE BARBARIAN

	CONAN O'BRIEN	CONAN THE BARBARIAN
Born in:	Brookline, MA	Cimmeria
Time slot:	11 p.m. EST (between *Family Guy* reruns and *Lopez Tonight*)	between the fall of Atlantis and recorded history
Early career:	lowly *Simpsons* writer	lowly thief and pirate
Replaced:	David Letterman	Kull the Conqueror
Hair:	riotous red	flowing
Physique:	pale and gangly	tan and jacked
Slays with:	rapier wit	swords and axes
Deposed by:	Jay Leno	an evil wizard
Religion:	Irish Catholic	Krom-Worship
Sidekick:	Andy Richter	hot girl in metal bikini

Screwed Up Life Lessons from Movies

// *Forrest Gump:*
ANYONE CAN BECOME RICH AND FAMOUS. EVEN YOU, STUPID.

// *The Little Mermaid:*
NEVER BE HAPPY WITH WHO YOU ARE.

// *Beauty and the Beast:*
IF YOU STICK WITH AN EMOTIONALLY ABUSIVE MAN LONG ENOUGH, HE'LL TOTALLY CHANGE.

// *Alice in Wonderland:*
EAT AND DRINK ANYTHING THAT IS PUT IN FRONT OF YOU.

// *Jurassic Park:*
SCIENCE CAN OPEN DOORS. TO EAT YOU.

// *Star Wars:*
ANCESTRY.COM IS WORTH THE MONEY.

// *Back to the Future:*
1985 WAS THE APEX OF HUMAN POTENTIAL.

// *WALL-E:*
FORCING YOURSELF ON A GIRL WHILE SHE IS UNCONSCIOUS LEADS TO LOVE.

// *Ferris Bueller's Day Off:*
IF YOU'RE REALLY POPULAR, YOU CAN DO WHATEVER YOU WANT.

// *The Lion King:*
CERTAIN RACES ARE MEANT TO RULE THE PLANET.

// *The Shining:*
THE FAMILY THAT VACAYS TOGETHER, STAYS TOGETHER. FOREVER.

IF THEY HAD BEEN RAPPERS

(Buster Keaton)
Busta Keaton / "Bullet for Chaplin"

(M. C. Escher)
MC Esher / "These Stairs Be Crazy!"

(Cleopatra)
Lil' Cleo / "Back That Asp Up"

(Frank Sinatra)
F. Sinny / "The Shorty Is a Skank"

(Fyvush Finkel)
5ish Finkel / "Yiddish 4 Life"

(Winston Churchill)
Bulldawg / "We Shall Fight on the Bitches"

(Ernest Hemingway)
Papa / "Old Man and the C Word"

(Marie Antoinette)
Queenie / "Eat My Cake"

(William Shakespeare)
will.i.am / "Much Ado about F*ckin"

(Walt Whitman)
Doubleyewandoubleyew / "Leaves of Ass"

(Benjamin Franklin)
Big Ben / "Healthy, Wealthy and Fly"

(Stephen Hawking)
Speak 'n' Spell / "A Brief History of Rhyme"

(Abraham Lincoln)
4 Score / "The Dance Nation Proclamation"

(Jane Goodall)
Ape Sh*t / "Hard Out Here for a Chimp"

(Henry VIII)
Ol' Dirty Heretic / "99 Problems but a Bitch Ain't Six"

THE BALDWINS

 **ALEC**

 **DANIEL**

 **WILLIAM**

 **STEPHEN**

	ALEC	DANIEL	WILLIAM	STEPHEN
POSITION IN FAMILY	Top Dog	Black Sheep	Forgotten	Christian One
POSITION IN LIFE	Mega Star	Rehab	He has many hobbies	*I'm a Celebrity… Get Me Out of Here!*
GOOD FRIENDS WITH	*The Huffington Post*	His parole officer	Kim Wayans	The Republican Party
BALDWIN HIGH	Marrying Kim Basinger	Having people realize that he's not Alec	Having people remember his existence	Still being famous for no real reason
BALDWIN LOW	Calling daughter a "thoughtless little pig" on voice mail	Getting arrested for the millionth time	Having people forget his existence	*Bio-Dome*
CAREER HIGH	*30 Rock*	*Homicide: Life on the Street*	*Backdraft*	*The Usual Suspects*
NEEDS TO WORK ON	Rage / snack issues	Hygiene	Alec Baldwin impressions	open-mindedness

VIDEO GAMES VS. REALITY

CALL OF DUTY

Your Game World: If you get 20 kills and 10 deaths in a round, you're doing pretty good.

Your Reality: Dying more than zero times is not good.

MARIO KART

Your Game World: Leaving a trail of banana peels behind you can help clinch a victory.

Your Reality: Littering from a moving vehicle: fine of up to $1,000.

SUPER MARIO

Your Game World: If you run around and stomp enough animals, you will get an extra life.

Your Reality: Animal cruelty is a felony.

WORLD OF WARCRAFT

Your Game World: You have friends across the whole world.

Your Reality: You haven't seen another living human in two weeks.

TETRIS

Your Game World: When you fill up four rows of bricks, they all disappear.

Your Reality: When you fill up four rows of bricks, you have built a wall.

BOMBERMAN

Your Game World: Bomberman is a hero.

Your Reality: Bomberman is a terrorist.

GRAND THEFT AUTO

Your Game World: You can run up to any car and pull the driver out.

Your Reality: People lock their car doors.

SONIC THE HEDGEHOG

Your Game World: You can zip across the landscape at dizzying speeds.

Your Reality: Hedgehogs are super slow.

MADDEN

Your Game World: You can win the Super Bowl.

Your Reality: You can't catch a ball.

Board Games in Real Life

Humanity's leisure-time relationship with board games goes back a ways. We've been playing them since before we had written languages (which may explain why we still have such an aversion to reading the rules for an unfamiliar game). We're even still playing some of these ancient games today—a backgammon set recently unearthed in Iran dates back to 3000 BC (Schädler and Ulrich 2010)

The first types of board games were abstract strategy competitions, like chess or checkers, and so-called race games, like backgammon or Parcheesi, in which players attempt to be the first to get their respective pieces to the end of the "track." As the centuries went by, games increasingly became more elaborate, involving backstories and often an extensive array of components (such as Monopoly's copious game pieces, deeds, cards, and money). The appeal of these games has always been their fantasy reflection of the real world, from subjects as serious as war to activities as commonplace as dating. Of course, these reflections are rarely very truthful.

IF BOARD GAMES WERE REALISTIC

GAME OF LIFE:
Extended period of living with your parents. Multiple marriages.

MONOPOLY:
Real estate fraud backed by the bank.

SETTLERS OF CATAN:
Trade two sheep for a disease-infected blanket.

CHESS:
All the pawns die and the Kings work out a treaty.

OPERATION:
Multiple malpractice lawsuits.

ROCK'EM SOCK'EM ROBOTS:
"Blue Bomber" taken down in a robo-steroid scandal.

CLUE:
Some thug. With the sawed-off. In a drive-by.

BATTLESHIP:
One player has a gigantic naval fleet, the other a single Somali pirate ship.

RISK:
One player spends more on their military than all the other players combined and loses.

CANDY-LAND:
Cavities.

MOVIE CHARACTER HEIGHT CHART

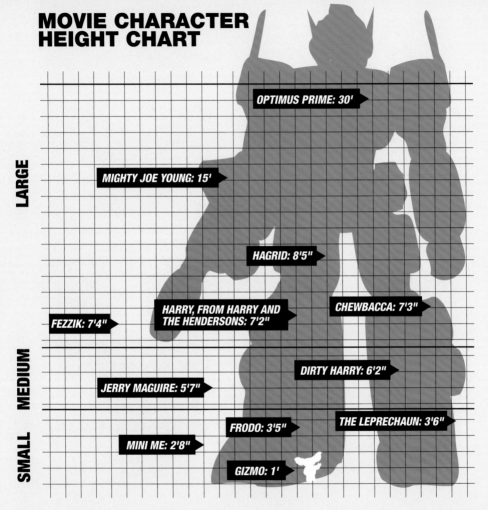

LARGE

MEDIUM

SMALL

OPTIMUS PRIME: 30'

MIGHTY JOE YOUNG: 15'

HAGRID: 8'5"

FEZZIK: 7'4"

HARRY, FROM HARRY AND THE HENDERSONS: 7'2"

CHEWBACCA: 7'3"

DIRTY HARRY: 6'2"

JERRY MAGUIRE: 5'7"

FRODO: 3'5"

THE LEPRECHAUN: 3'6"

MINI ME: 2'8"

GIZMO: 1'

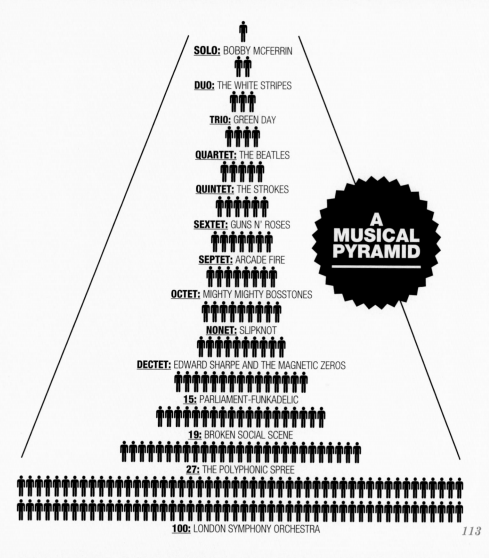

SOLO: BOBBY MCFERRIN

DUO: THE WHITE STRIPES

TRIO: GREEN DAY

QUARTET: THE BEATLES

QUINTET: THE STROKES

SEXTET: GUNS N' ROSES

SEPTET: ARCADE FIRE

OCTET: MIGHTY MIGHTY BOSSTONES

NONET: SLIPKNOT

DECTET: EDWARD SHARPE AND THE MAGNETIC ZEROS

15: PARLIAMENT-FUNKADELIC

19: BROKEN SOCIAL SCENE

27: THE POLYPHONIC SPREE

100: LONDON SYMPHONY ORCHESTRA

A MUSICAL PYRAMID

THE HIERARCHY OF BLACK ROYALTY IN THE UNITED STATES (BY NAME)

THE ROYAL FAMILY

B.B. King
&
Queen Latifah

Prince & Princess

THE COURT

Duke Ellington

Count Basie & Countess Vaughn

Baron Davis

Earl the Pearl Monroe

Sir Mix-a-Lot & Suge Knight

Lady Saw

Ornette "The Court Jester" Coleman

WORLD-FAMOUS ORPHANS →	BATMAN	TARZAN	SIMBA
PARENTS' FATE:	Murdered by a mugger	Murdered by apes	Murdered by Scar
RAISED BY:	Alfred, the butler	Kala, an ape	A hetero-lifemate coupling of a meerkat and warthog
DISCOVERED HIS POTENTIAL WHEN:	He fell into a bat cave.	He found out he's human.	He hallucinated.
SOURCE OF POWERS:	He's superdetermined. And rich.	He was raised in the jungle. By apes.	He's a lion.
ARCH NEMESIS:	The Joker	Shirts	Scar

Corpse Disposal in Hollywood

Humans are not the only animals to engage in funerary acts—elephants have been known to lay branches and leaves over their dead—but we definitely have the most complex variety of practices for consigning our deceased to the hereafter. The earliest undisputed human burial was discovered by archaeologists in Israel and dates back 130,000 years (Lieberman 1991). Interment in the ground remains the most popular option for what to do with a corpse, but the modern bereaved American now has a host of options from a diverse assortment of cultures and belief systems.

DISTRIBUTION OF COMMON CORPSE DISPOSAL:

HOLLYWOOD, CALIFORNIA 90029

53% VIKING FUNERAL PYRE

8% BURIAL

2% CREMATION

26% EATEN BY STARVING SOCCER TEAM

3% EATEN BY PIGS

5% BURIAL AT SEA

3% DONATED TO SCIENCE

Monster Cereals

Ancient farmers first domesticated cereal grains around 10,000 BC in the Fertile Crescent region of the Middle East, though modern-day "breakfast cereal" did not appear until the latter half of the nineteenth

 century, spurred by a wave of popularity for vegetarianism. Will Keith Kellogg was not the first to individually box breakfast cereals, but his Kellogg's Corn Flakes became the first cereal to catch on nationwide in a big way (Flynn 2002). After World War II, the major cereal companies began marketing toward children, convincing mothers everywhere that cereal was a balanced part of every breakfast.

The ancient Greeks believed that the goddess Echidna was the "Mother of All Monsters." Like any mother, her children surely each had their favorites to add to her grocery list.

Monster	Cereal
DRACULA	COUNT CHOCULA
FRANKENSTEIN'S MONSTER	FRANKEN BERRY
WOLF MAN	FRUIT BRUTE
MUMMY	YUMMY MUMMY
CREATURE FROM THE BLACK LAGOON	CAP'N CRUNCH'S DEEP-SEA CRUNCH
INVISIBLE MAN	KASHI GO LEAN
KING KONG	SUPER BANANA CRISP
DR. JEKYLL & MR. HYDE	FROSTED MINI-WHEATS

CLASSIC MONSTERS' FAVORITE CEREAL

BIBLIOGRAPHY

Bradbey, Sara. 2009. "A Picture Is Worth a Thousand Lies." *Modern Person*.

Calentori, Giuseppe. 1915. "Study of My Wife and Abnormal Aggression." *Corriere della Sera*.

Darwin, Charles. 1871. *The Descent of Man and Selection in Relation to Sex*. 2004 ed. Kessinger Publishing.

Driscoll, C. A., D. W. MacDonald, and S. J. O'Brien. 2009. "In the Light of Evolution III: Two Centuries of Darwin Sackler Colloquium: From Wild Animals to Domestic Pets, an Evolutionary View of Domestication". *Proceedings of the National Academy of Sciences of the United States of America*.

Erinsen, Lars. 1999. "Are Scientists Boring?" *Popular Science*.

Flynn, Maxwell. 2002. "The Long Exciting History of Breakfast Cereal." *Cereal Monthly*.

Hughes, Geoffrey. 2000. *A History of English Words*. Blackwell Publishing.

Lieberman, Phillip. 1991. *Uniquely Human*. Harvard University Press.

Magnello, M. E. 1856. "Karl Pearson and the Origins of Modern Statistics: An Elastician Becomes a Statistician." *The New Zealand Journal for the History and Philosophy of Science and Technology*.

McCarthy, Cormac. 2006. *The Road*. New York: Alfred A. Knopf.

Page, Turner and Harry Shapiro. 1927. *Women, What Are They? A Critical Study by Man*. Minneapolis, MN: University of Minneapolis Press.

Patton, George S. 1944. "Speech to the Third Army," transcript.

Playfair, William. 1804. *More Statistical Breviary*. 1977 ed. Oxford: Oxford University Press.

Post, Edward. 1935. *Frank Bunker Gilbreth Sr.* Mullen Press.

Ramon, Elizabeth. 1982. *All the Cool Cultures Are Doing It*. Wydman Publishing.

Savolainen P, Y. P. Zhang, J. Luo, J. Lundeberg, and T. Leitner. 2002. "Genetic Evidence for an East Asian Origin of Domestic Dogs." *Science*.

Schädler, Dunn-Vaturi, and Anne-Elizabeth Ulrich. 2010. "Board Games in Pre-Islamic Persia," *Encyclopædia Iranica*.

Scurr, Dr. Joanna. 2011. "Unnamed Boob Study." PhD diss. University of Portsmouth.

Stellman, Aaron and Margo Piper. 1991. *Music and the Mind*. Porter Hound Press.

Sun Tzu. [500 BC?] *The Art of War*.

Swartzwelder, John. 1997. "Homer Versus the 18th Amendment." *The Simpsons*.

Zytho, Arus. 1955. "Pie Versus Cake: The History Battle." *Greek Science*. Athens Central Press.

OTHER ULYSSES PRESS BOOKS

A Zombie's History of the United States: From the Massacre at Plymouth Rock to the CIA's Secret War on the Undead
Dr. Worm Miller, $13.95
After years of stealthy research in the vaults of the CIA and the FBI, the author of this shocking book provides disturbing proof that centuries of systematic suppression have kept secret the darkest truth of America's past. Now someone has finally brought to light the 500-year history of America's most invisible minority: zombies.

Married to the Sea: Victorian Newspaper Art Gone Wrong
Drew, $14.95
Reinventing the single-panel cartoon for today's hippest readers, *Married to the Sea* applies modern American culture to stodgy Victorian characters with bizarrely funny results. The author's shocking captions lay bare the gulf between today and the Victorian era.

I Call Bullshit: Debunking the Most Commonly Repeated Myths
Jamie Frater, $13.95
Dissecting the myths, misconceptions, and all-out lies that almost everyone believes as "fact," *I Call Bullshit* will shock and amaze readers with just how much trivia they have wrong.

Listverse.com's Ultimate Book of Bizarre Lists
Jamie Frater, $15.95
Delving into the strange side of pop culture, this book offers lists such as death-related objects available for purchase online; the weirdest things Michael Jackson owned; strange occupations like a "knocker-up"; and the most interesting creatures in Japanese folklore.

To order these books call 800-377-2542 or 510-601-8301, fax 510-601-8307, e-mail ulysses@ulyssespress.com, or write to Ulysses Press, P.O. Box 3440, Berkeley, CA 94703. All retail orders are shipped free of charge. California residents must include sales tax. Allow two to three weeks for delivery.

ABOUT THE AUTHORS

PATRICK CASEY grew up in Bloomington, Minnesota. After receiving his degree from Boston University, he moved to Hollywood, California, where he currently resides with his cat. He sometimes does things that make other humans laugh.

WORM MILLER also grew up in Bloomington, Minnesota. When not working as a writer, he is training to become a handsome, emotionally complex international jewel thief and someday hopes to horribly regret putting that information in a book bio.